# THE BEAST GYM DIARY

To get bigger, stronger and better... `
power that earned me the title of W
tive thinking, staying focused and trair.. ᵧ /

Your mind set and organisation is just as important as the great feeling you get *"Throwing those weights around"*. You need to be organised and have a game plan… If you want gains, you need to continuously up your game and lift more!

Using a clever and organised Gym Diary to track your progress is a key factor to *"Moving forever forward"*. Especially if it's laid out like **My Gym Diary**. See your progress on a single page… Know what you lifted last week, the previous week and the weeks before that. See your results unfold week to week… Up your game and lift more…

Using my Gym Diary Format will push you forward…

Look at your exercise log page before your workout and you will know -

**"It's time to get to work!"**

*This book is "Perfect Bound" meaning the spine is glued. It allows us to get more pages into a small space - which is a good thing! As your Diary is straight off the press it may feel stiff, so to assure you it's going to work well in the gym, turn, thumb and fold each page to loosen it up a bit - "Don't worry you can't break it".*

Authors: Eddie Hall, John Bowers
Printed by Amazon ISBN No. See back cover
© Copyright 2017 The Beast Ltd & Sets, Reps & Done!

# HOW TO SET UP YOUR GYM DIARY

## ONE **EXERCISE** - ONE **PAGE**...!

This is a more logical layout and allows you to see all your results on one page! And this is the key information you **NEED** to be **SEEING** if you want to keep making progress and get bigger and better gains!

It's a real **GOAL SETTER**... Seeing the history of your exercise results in this format will really push you forward!

Pop the date in this end and move across **BOTH** pages...
One **Row** is one **Day** - unless you do more then 7 Sets per Exercise.
If you do, simply continue to use the next row.

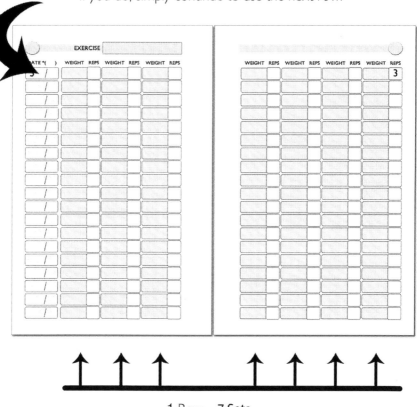

1 Row = 7 Sets

DATE *(   )
Enter year if required

## CREATE YOUR **OWN** EXERCISE INDEX...

You choose which exercise goes on what page. Of course you can use the same exercises for more than one page if you need too.

There are 40 pages - enough for anyone!

Suggested - Work around your body in a logical order, Forearms, Biceps, Triceps, Shoulders and so on…

If you fill up a page, you can use more than one page for the same exercise.

Once you have created your index, you can set about building your regular routines or set up some new ones!

## **YOUR** ROUTINES

Give your routine a name or reference -
Example -  **LEG DAY**….

Simply create your routine and write the page number for your Exercise, referring to your Exercise Index page.

\* Your Routine pages are to
be found at the back.

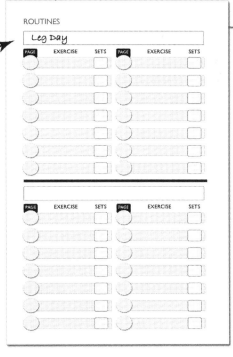

 **DONE!**
It's time to get to work!

# EXERCISE INDEX

1

2

3

4

5

6

7

8

9

10

11

12

13

14

15

16

17

18

19

20

## Protein Dynamix

21

22

23

24

25

26

27

28

29

30

31

32

33

34

35

36

37

38

39

40

# Eddie
# Hall

KEEP UP TO DATE

My Schedule, My Routines, My Results, My Offers!

www.eddiehallstrongman.com

**1** EXERCISE

| DATE *( ) | WEIGHT | REPS | WEIGHT | REPS | WEIGHT | REPS |
|---|---|---|---|---|---|---|
| / | | | | | | |
| / | | | | | | |
| / | | | | | | |
| / | | | | | | |
| / | | | | | | |
| / | | | | | | |
| / | | | | | | |
| / | | | | | | |
| / | | | | | | |
| / | | | | | | |
| / | | | | | | |
| / | | | | | | |
| / | | | | | | |
| / | | | | | | |
| / | | | | | | |
| / | | | | | | |
| / | | | | | | |
| / | | | | | | |
| / | | | | | | |

| WEIGHT | REPS | WEIGHT | REPS | WEIGHT | REPS | WEIGHT | REPS |
|--------|------|--------|------|--------|------|--------|------|
|        |      |        |      |        |      |        |      |
|        |      |        |      |        |      |        |      |
|        |      |        |      |        |      |        |      |
|        |      |        |      |        |      |        |      |
|        |      |        |      |        |      |        |      |
|        |      |        |      |        |      |        |      |
|        |      |        |      |        |      |        |      |
|        |      |        |      |        |      |        |      |
|        |      |        |      |        |      |        |      |
|        |      |        |      |        |      |        |      |
|        |      |        |      |        |      |        |      |
|        |      |        |      |        |      |        |      |
|        |      |        |      |        |      |        |      |
|        |      |        |      |        |      |        |      |
|        |      |        |      |        |      |        |      |
|        |      |        |      |        |      |        |      |
|        |      |        |      |        |      |        |      |
|        |      |        |      |        |      |        |      |
|        |      |        |      |        |      |        |      |

## 2 EXERCISE

| DATE *( ) | WEIGHT | REPS | WEIGHT | REPS | WEIGHT | REPS |
|---|---|---|---|---|---|---|
| / | | | | | | |
| / | | | | | | |
| / | | | | | | |
| / | | | | | | |
| / | | | | | | |
| / | | | | | | |
| / | | | | | | |
| / | | | | | | |
| / | | | | | | |
| / | | | | | | |
| / | | | | | | |
| / | | | | | | |
| / | | | | | | |
| / | | | | | | |
| / | | | | | | |
| / | | | | | | |
| / | | | | | | |
| / | | | | | | |
| / | | | | | | |

| WEIGHT | REPS | WEIGHT | REPS | WEIGHT | REPS | WEIGHT | REPS |
|---|---|---|---|---|---|---|---|
|  |  |  |  |  |  |  |  |
|  |  |  |  |  |  |  |  |
|  |  |  |  |  |  |  |  |
|  |  |  |  |  |  |  |  |
|  |  |  |  |  |  |  |  |
|  |  |  |  |  |  |  |  |
|  |  |  |  |  |  |  |  |
|  |  |  |  |  |  |  |  |
|  |  |  |  |  |  |  |  |
|  |  |  |  |  |  |  |  |
|  |  |  |  |  |  |  |  |
|  |  |  |  |  |  |  |  |
|  |  |  |  |  |  |  |  |
|  |  |  |  |  |  |  |  |
|  |  |  |  |  |  |  |  |
|  |  |  |  |  |  |  |  |
|  |  |  |  |  |  |  |  |
|  |  |  |  |  |  |  |  |
|  |  |  |  |  |  |  |  |

## 3     EXERCISE

| DATE *( ) | WEIGHT | REPS | WEIGHT | REPS | WEIGHT | REPS |
|-----------|--------|------|--------|------|--------|------|
| / | | | | | | |
| / | | | | | | |
| / | | | | | | |
| / | | | | | | |
| / | | | | | | |
| / | | | | | | |
| / | | | | | | |
| / | | | | | | |
| / | | | | | | |
| / | | | | | | |
| / | | | | | | |
| / | | | | | | |
| / | | | | | | |
| / | | | | | | |
| / | | | | | | |
| / | | | | | | |
| / | | | | | | |
| / | | | | | | |
| / | | | | | | |

| WEIGHT | REPS | WEIGHT | REPS | WEIGHT | REPS | WEIGHT | REPS |
|---|---|---|---|---|---|---|---|
|  |  |  |  |  |  |  |  |
|  |  |  |  |  |  |  |  |
|  |  |  |  |  |  |  |  |
|  |  |  |  |  |  |  |  |
|  |  |  |  |  |  |  |  |
|  |  |  |  |  |  |  |  |
|  |  |  |  |  |  |  |  |
|  |  |  |  |  |  |  |  |
|  |  |  |  |  |  |  |  |
|  |  |  |  |  |  |  |  |
|  |  |  |  |  |  |  |  |
|  |  |  |  |  |  |  |  |
|  |  |  |  |  |  |  |  |
|  |  |  |  |  |  |  |  |
|  |  |  |  |  |  |  |  |
|  |  |  |  |  |  |  |  |
|  |  |  |  |  |  |  |  |
|  |  |  |  |  |  |  |  |
|  |  |  |  |  |  |  |  |

## 4     EXERCISE

| DATE *( ) | WEIGHT | REPS | WEIGHT | REPS | WEIGHT | REPS |
|-----------|--------|------|--------|------|--------|------|
| / | | | | | | |
| / | | | | | | |
| / | | | | | | |
| / | | | | | | |
| / | | | | | | |
| / | | | | | | |
| / | | | | | | |
| / | | | | | | |
| / | | | | | | |
| / | | | | | | |
| / | | | | | | |
| / | | | | | | |
| / | | | | | | |
| / | | | | | | |
| / | | | | | | |
| / | | | | | | |
| / | | | | | | |
| / | | | | | | |
| / | | | | | | |

| WEIGHT | REPS | WEIGHT | REPS | WEIGHT | REPS | WEIGHT | REPS |
|--------|------|--------|------|--------|------|--------|------|
|        |      |        |      |        |      |        |      |
|        |      |        |      |        |      |        |      |
|        |      |        |      |        |      |        |      |
|        |      |        |      |        |      |        |      |
|        |      |        |      |        |      |        |      |
|        |      |        |      |        |      |        |      |
|        |      |        |      |        |      |        |      |
|        |      |        |      |        |      |        |      |
|        |      |        |      |        |      |        |      |
|        |      |        |      |        |      |        |      |
|        |      |        |      |        |      |        |      |
|        |      |        |      |        |      |        |      |
|        |      |        |      |        |      |        |      |
|        |      |        |      |        |      |        |      |
|        |      |        |      |        |      |        |      |
|        |      |        |      |        |      |        |      |
|        |      |        |      |        |      |        |      |
|        |      |        |      |        |      |        |      |
|        |      |        |      |        |      |        |      |

## 5 EXERCISE

| DATE *( ) | WEIGHT | REPS | WEIGHT | REPS | WEIGHT | REPS |
|---|---|---|---|---|---|---|
| / | | | | | | |
| / | | | | | | |
| / | | | | | | |
| / | | | | | | |
| / | | | | | | |
| / | | | | | | |
| / | | | | | | |
| / | | | | | | |
| / | | | | | | |
| / | | | | | | |
| / | | | | | | |
| / | | | | | | |
| / | | | | | | |
| / | | | | | | |
| / | | | | | | |
| / | | | | | | |
| / | | | | | | |
| / | | | | | | |
| / | | | | | | |

| WEIGHT | REPS | WEIGHT | REPS | WEIGHT | REPS | WEIGHT | REPS |
|---|---|---|---|---|---|---|---|
|  |  |  |  |  |  |  |  |
|  |  |  |  |  |  |  |  |
|  |  |  |  |  |  |  |  |
|  |  |  |  |  |  |  |  |
|  |  |  |  |  |  |  |  |
|  |  |  |  |  |  |  |  |
|  |  |  |  |  |  |  |  |
|  |  |  |  |  |  |  |  |
|  |  |  |  |  |  |  |  |
|  |  |  |  |  |  |  |  |
|  |  |  |  |  |  |  |  |
|  |  |  |  |  |  |  |  |
|  |  |  |  |  |  |  |  |
|  |  |  |  |  |  |  |  |
|  |  |  |  |  |  |  |  |
|  |  |  |  |  |  |  |  |
|  |  |  |  |  |  |  |  |
|  |  |  |  |  |  |  |  |
|  |  |  |  |  |  |  |  |

**6** EXERCISE

| DATE *(   ) | WEIGHT | REPS | WEIGHT | REPS | WEIGHT | REPS |
|---|---|---|---|---|---|---|
| / | | | | | | |
| / | | | | | | |
| / | | | | | | |
| / | | | | | | |
| / | | | | | | |
| / | | | | | | |
| / | | | | | | |
| / | | | | | | |
| / | | | | | | |
| / | | | | | | |
| / | | | | | | |
| / | | | | | | |
| / | | | | | | |
| / | | | | | | |
| / | | | | | | |
| / | | | | | | |
| / | | | | | | |
| / | | | | | | |
| / | | | | | | |

| WEIGHT | REPS | WEIGHT | REPS | WEIGHT | REPS | WEIGHT | REPS |
|---|---|---|---|---|---|---|---|
|  |  |  |  |  |  |  |  |
|  |  |  |  |  |  |  |  |
|  |  |  |  |  |  |  |  |
|  |  |  |  |  |  |  |  |
|  |  |  |  |  |  |  |  |
|  |  |  |  |  |  |  |  |
|  |  |  |  |  |  |  |  |
|  |  |  |  |  |  |  |  |
|  |  |  |  |  |  |  |  |
|  |  |  |  |  |  |  |  |
|  |  |  |  |  |  |  |  |
|  |  |  |  |  |  |  |  |
|  |  |  |  |  |  |  |  |
|  |  |  |  |  |  |  |  |
|  |  |  |  |  |  |  |  |
|  |  |  |  |  |  |  |  |
|  |  |  |  |  |  |  |  |
|  |  |  |  |  |  |  |  |
|  |  |  |  |  |  |  |  |

## 7 EXERCISE

| DATE *(  ) | WEIGHT | REPS | WEIGHT | REPS | WEIGHT | REPS |
|---|---|---|---|---|---|---|
| / | | | | | | |
| / | | | | | | |
| / | | | | | | |
| / | | | | | | |
| / | | | | | | |
| / | | | | | | |
| / | | | | | | |
| / | | | | | | |
| / | | | | | | |
| / | | | | | | |
| / | | | | | | |
| / | | | | | | |
| / | | | | | | |
| / | | | | | | |
| / | | | | | | |
| / | | | | | | |
| / | | | | | | |
| / | | | | | | |
| / | | | | | | |

| WEIGHT | REPS | WEIGHT | REPS | WEIGHT | REPS | WEIGHT | REPS |
|---|---|---|---|---|---|---|---|
| | | | | | | | |
| | | | | | | | |
| | | | | | | | |
| | | | | | | | |
| | | | | | | | |
| | | | | | | | |
| | | | | | | | |
| | | | | | | | |
| | | | | | | | |
| | | | | | | | |
| | | | | | | | |
| | | | | | | | |
| | | | | | | | |
| | | | | | | | |
| | | | | | | | |
| | | | | | | | |
| | | | | | | | |
| | | | | | | | |
| | | | | | | | |

## 8 EXERCISE

| DATE *(  ) | WEIGHT | REPS | WEIGHT | REPS | WEIGHT | REPS |
|---|---|---|---|---|---|---|
| / | | | | | | |
| / | | | | | | |
| / | | | | | | |
| / | | | | | | |
| / | | | | | | |
| / | | | | | | |
| / | | | | | | |
| / | | | | | | |
| / | | | | | | |
| / | | | | | | |
| / | | | | | | |
| / | | | | | | |
| / | | | | | | |
| / | | | | | | |
| / | | | | | | |
| / | | | | | | |
| / | | | | | | |
| / | | | | | | |
| / | | | | | | |

| WEIGHT | REPS | WEIGHT | REPS | WEIGHT | REPS | WEIGHT | REPS |
|--------|------|--------|------|--------|------|--------|------|
|        |      |        |      |        |      |        |      |
|        |      |        |      |        |      |        |      |
|        |      |        |      |        |      |        |      |
|        |      |        |      |        |      |        |      |
|        |      |        |      |        |      |        |      |
|        |      |        |      |        |      |        |      |
|        |      |        |      |        |      |        |      |
|        |      |        |      |        |      |        |      |
|        |      |        |      |        |      |        |      |
|        |      |        |      |        |      |        |      |
|        |      |        |      |        |      |        |      |
|        |      |        |      |        |      |        |      |
|        |      |        |      |        |      |        |      |
|        |      |        |      |        |      |        |      |
|        |      |        |      |        |      |        |      |
|        |      |        |      |        |      |        |      |
|        |      |        |      |        |      |        |      |
|        |      |        |      |        |      |        |      |
|        |      |        |      |        |      |        |      |

**9**      EXERCISE

| DATE *(  ) | WEIGHT | REPS | WEIGHT | REPS | WEIGHT | REPS |
|---|---|---|---|---|---|---|
| / | | | | | | |
| / | | | | | | |
| / | | | | | | |
| / | | | | | | |
| / | | | | | | |
| / | | | | | | |
| / | | | | | | |
| / | | | | | | |
| / | | | | | | |
| / | | | | | | |
| / | | | | | | |
| / | | | | | | |
| / | | | | | | |
| / | | | | | | |
| / | | | | | | |
| / | | | | | | |
| / | | | | | | |
| / | | | | | | |
| / | | | | | | |

| WEIGHT | REPS | WEIGHT | REPS | WEIGHT | REPS | WEIGHT | REPS |
|--------|------|--------|------|--------|------|--------|------|
|        |      |        |      |        |      |        |      |
|        |      |        |      |        |      |        |      |
|        |      |        |      |        |      |        |      |
|        |      |        |      |        |      |        |      |
|        |      |        |      |        |      |        |      |
|        |      |        |      |        |      |        |      |
|        |      |        |      |        |      |        |      |
|        |      |        |      |        |      |        |      |
|        |      |        |      |        |      |        |      |
|        |      |        |      |        |      |        |      |
|        |      |        |      |        |      |        |      |
|        |      |        |      |        |      |        |      |
|        |      |        |      |        |      |        |      |
|        |      |        |      |        |      |        |      |
|        |      |        |      |        |      |        |      |
|        |      |        |      |        |      |        |      |
|        |      |        |      |        |      |        |      |
|        |      |        |      |        |      |        |      |
|        |      |        |      |        |      |        |      |

## 10 EXERCISE

| DATE *( ) | WEIGHT | REPS | WEIGHT | REPS | WEIGHT | REPS |
|-----------|--------|------|--------|------|--------|------|
| / | | | | | | |
| / | | | | | | |
| / | | | | | | |
| / | | | | | | |
| / | | | | | | |
| / | | | | | | |
| / | | | | | | |
| / | | | | | | |
| / | | | | | | |
| / | | | | | | |
| / | | | | | | |
| / | | | | | | |
| / | | | | | | |
| / | | | | | | |
| / | | | | | | |
| / | | | | | | |
| / | | | | | | |
| / | | | | | | |
| / | | | | | | |

| WEIGHT | REPS | WEIGHT | REPS | WEIGHT | REPS | WEIGHT | REPS |
|---|---|---|---|---|---|---|---|
|  |  |  |  |  |  |  |  |
|  |  |  |  |  |  |  |  |
|  |  |  |  |  |  |  |  |
|  |  |  |  |  |  |  |  |
|  |  |  |  |  |  |  |  |
|  |  |  |  |  |  |  |  |
|  |  |  |  |  |  |  |  |
|  |  |  |  |  |  |  |  |
|  |  |  |  |  |  |  |  |
|  |  |  |  |  |  |  |  |
|  |  |  |  |  |  |  |  |
|  |  |  |  |  |  |  |  |
|  |  |  |  |  |  |  |  |
|  |  |  |  |  |  |  |  |
|  |  |  |  |  |  |  |  |
|  |  |  |  |  |  |  |  |
|  |  |  |  |  |  |  |  |
|  |  |  |  |  |  |  |  |
|  |  |  |  |  |  |  |  |

## 11 EXERCISE

| DATE *( ) | WEIGHT | REPS | WEIGHT | REPS | WEIGHT | REPS |
|---|---|---|---|---|---|---|
| / | | | | | | |
| / | | | | | | |
| / | | | | | | |
| / | | | | | | |
| / | | | | | | |
| / | | | | | | |
| / | | | | | | |
| / | | | | | | |
| / | | | | | | |
| / | | | | | | |
| / | | | | | | |
| / | | | | | | |
| / | | | | | | |
| / | | | | | | |
| / | | | | | | |
| / | | | | | | |
| / | | | | | | |
| / | | | | | | |
| / | | | | | | |

| WEIGHT | REPS | WEIGHT | REPS | WEIGHT | REPS | WEIGHT | REPS |
|---|---|---|---|---|---|---|---|
|  |  |  |  |  |  |  |  |
|  |  |  |  |  |  |  |  |
|  |  |  |  |  |  |  |  |
|  |  |  |  |  |  |  |  |
|  |  |  |  |  |  |  |  |
|  |  |  |  |  |  |  |  |
|  |  |  |  |  |  |  |  |
|  |  |  |  |  |  |  |  |
|  |  |  |  |  |  |  |  |
|  |  |  |  |  |  |  |  |
|  |  |  |  |  |  |  |  |
|  |  |  |  |  |  |  |  |
|  |  |  |  |  |  |  |  |
|  |  |  |  |  |  |  |  |
|  |  |  |  |  |  |  |  |
|  |  |  |  |  |  |  |  |
|  |  |  |  |  |  |  |  |
|  |  |  |  |  |  |  |  |
|  |  |  |  |  |  |  |  |

## 12

EXERCISE

| DATE *( ) | WEIGHT | REPS | WEIGHT | REPS | WEIGHT | REPS |
|-----------|--------|------|--------|------|--------|------|
| / | | | | | | |
| / | | | | | | |
| / | | | | | | |
| / | | | | | | |
| / | | | | | | |
| / | | | | | | |
| / | | | | | | |
| / | | | | | | |
| / | | | | | | |
| / | | | | | | |
| / | | | | | | |
| / | | | | | | |
| / | | | | | | |
| / | | | | | | |
| / | | | | | | |
| / | | | | | | |
| / | | | | | | |
| / | | | | | | |
| / | | | | | | |

| WEIGHT | REPS | WEIGHT | REPS | WEIGHT | REPS | WEIGHT | REPS |
|---|---|---|---|---|---|---|---|
| | | | | | | | |
| | | | | | | | |
| | | | | | | | |
| | | | | | | | |
| | | | | | | | |
| | | | | | | | |
| | | | | | | | |
| | | | | | | | |
| | | | | | | | |
| | | | | | | | |
| | | | | | | | |
| | | | | | | | |
| | | | | | | | |
| | | | | | | | |
| | | | | | | | |
| | | | | | | | |
| | | | | | | | |
| | | | | | | | |
| | | | | | | | |

## 13 EXERCISE

| DATE *(  ) | WEIGHT | REPS | WEIGHT | REPS | WEIGHT | REPS |
|---|---|---|---|---|---|---|
| / | | | | | | |
| / | | | | | | |
| / | | | | | | |
| / | | | | | | |
| / | | | | | | |
| / | | | | | | |
| / | | | | | | |
| / | | | | | | |
| / | | | | | | |
| / | | | | | | |
| / | | | | | | |
| / | | | | | | |
| / | | | | | | |
| / | | | | | | |
| / | | | | | | |
| / | | | | | | |
| / | | | | | | |
| / | | | | | | |
| / | | | | | | |

| WEIGHT | REPS | WEIGHT | REPS | WEIGHT | REPS | WEIGHT | REPS |
|--------|------|--------|------|--------|------|--------|------|
|  |  |  |  |  |  |  |  |
|  |  |  |  |  |  |  |  |
|  |  |  |  |  |  |  |  |
|  |  |  |  |  |  |  |  |
|  |  |  |  |  |  |  |  |
|  |  |  |  |  |  |  |  |
|  |  |  |  |  |  |  |  |
|  |  |  |  |  |  |  |  |
|  |  |  |  |  |  |  |  |
|  |  |  |  |  |  |  |  |
|  |  |  |  |  |  |  |  |
|  |  |  |  |  |  |  |  |
|  |  |  |  |  |  |  |  |
|  |  |  |  |  |  |  |  |
|  |  |  |  |  |  |  |  |
|  |  |  |  |  |  |  |  |
|  |  |  |  |  |  |  |  |
|  |  |  |  |  |  |  |  |
|  |  |  |  |  |  |  |  |

## 14 EXERCISE

| DATE *(   ) | WEIGHT | REPS | WEIGHT | REPS | WEIGHT | REPS |
|---|---|---|---|---|---|---|
| / | | | | | | |
| / | | | | | | |
| / | | | | | | |
| / | | | | | | |
| / | | | | | | |
| / | | | | | | |
| / | | | | | | |
| / | | | | | | |
| / | | | | | | |
| / | | | | | | |
| / | | | | | | |
| / | | | | | | |
| / | | | | | | |
| / | | | | | | |
| / | | | | | | |
| / | | | | | | |
| / | | | | | | |
| / | | | | | | |
| / | | | | | | |

| WEIGHT | REPS | WEIGHT | REPS | WEIGHT | REPS | WEIGHT | REPS |
|---|---|---|---|---|---|---|---|
| | | | | | | | |
| | | | | | | | |
| | | | | | | | |
| | | | | | | | |
| | | | | | | | |
| | | | | | | | |
| | | | | | | | |
| | | | | | | | |
| | | | | | | | |
| | | | | | | | |
| | | | | | | | |
| | | | | | | | |
| | | | | | | | |
| | | | | | | | |
| | | | | | | | |
| | | | | | | | |
| | | | | | | | |
| | | | | | | | |
| | | | | | | | |

## 15 EXERCISE

| DATE *( ) | WEIGHT | REPS | WEIGHT | REPS | WEIGHT | REPS |
|-----------|--------|------|--------|------|--------|------|
| / | | | | | | |
| / | | | | | | |
| / | | | | | | |
| / | | | | | | |
| / | | | | | | |
| / | | | | | | |
| / | | | | | | |
| / | | | | | | |
| / | | | | | | |
| / | | | | | | |
| / | | | | | | |
| / | | | | | | |
| / | | | | | | |
| / | | | | | | |
| / | | | | | | |
| / | | | | | | |
| / | | | | | | |
| / | | | | | | |
| / | | | | | | |

| WEIGHT | REPS | WEIGHT | REPS | WEIGHT | REPS | WEIGHT | REPS |
|---|---|---|---|---|---|---|---|
| | | | | | | | |
| | | | | | | | |
| | | | | | | | |
| | | | | | | | |
| | | | | | | | |
| | | | | | | | |
| | | | | | | | |
| | | | | | | | |
| | | | | | | | |
| | | | | | | | |
| | | | | | | | |
| | | | | | | | |
| | | | | | | | |
| | | | | | | | |
| | | | | | | | |
| | | | | | | | |
| | | | | | | | |
| | | | | | | | |
| | | | | | | | |

## 16 EXERCISE

| DATE *(  ) | WEIGHT | REPS | WEIGHT | REPS | WEIGHT | REPS |
|---|---|---|---|---|---|---|
| / | | | | | | |
| / | | | | | | |
| / | | | | | | |
| / | | | | | | |
| / | | | | | | |
| / | | | | | | |
| / | | | | | | |
| / | | | | | | |
| / | | | | | | |
| / | | | | | | |
| / | | | | | | |
| / | | | | | | |
| / | | | | | | |
| / | | | | | | |
| / | | | | | | |
| / | | | | | | |
| / | | | | | | |
| / | | | | | | |
| / | | | | | | |

| WEIGHT | REPS | WEIGHT | REPS | WEIGHT | REPS | WEIGHT | REPS |
|---|---|---|---|---|---|---|---|
|  |  |  |  |  |  |  |  |
|  |  |  |  |  |  |  |  |
|  |  |  |  |  |  |  |  |
|  |  |  |  |  |  |  |  |
|  |  |  |  |  |  |  |  |
|  |  |  |  |  |  |  |  |
|  |  |  |  |  |  |  |  |
|  |  |  |  |  |  |  |  |
|  |  |  |  |  |  |  |  |
|  |  |  |  |  |  |  |  |
|  |  |  |  |  |  |  |  |
|  |  |  |  |  |  |  |  |
|  |  |  |  |  |  |  |  |
|  |  |  |  |  |  |  |  |
|  |  |  |  |  |  |  |  |
|  |  |  |  |  |  |  |  |
|  |  |  |  |  |  |  |  |
|  |  |  |  |  |  |  |  |
|  |  |  |  |  |  |  |  |

## 17 EXERCISE

| DATE *( ) | WEIGHT | REPS | WEIGHT | REPS | WEIGHT | REPS |
|-----------|--------|------|--------|------|--------|------|
| / | | | | | | |
| / | | | | | | |
| / | | | | | | |
| / | | | | | | |
| / | | | | | | |
| / | | | | | | |
| / | | | | | | |
| / | | | | | | |
| / | | | | | | |
| / | | | | | | |
| / | | | | | | |
| / | | | | | | |
| / | | | | | | |
| / | | | | | | |
| / | | | | | | |
| / | | | | | | |
| / | | | | | | |
| / | | | | | | |
| / | | | | | | |

| WEIGHT | REPS | WEIGHT | REPS | WEIGHT | REPS | WEIGHT | REPS |
|---|---|---|---|---|---|---|---|
|  |  |  |  |  |  |  |  |
|  |  |  |  |  |  |  |  |
|  |  |  |  |  |  |  |  |
|  |  |  |  |  |  |  |  |
|  |  |  |  |  |  |  |  |
|  |  |  |  |  |  |  |  |
|  |  |  |  |  |  |  |  |
|  |  |  |  |  |  |  |  |
|  |  |  |  |  |  |  |  |
|  |  |  |  |  |  |  |  |
|  |  |  |  |  |  |  |  |
|  |  |  |  |  |  |  |  |
|  |  |  |  |  |  |  |  |
|  |  |  |  |  |  |  |  |
|  |  |  |  |  |  |  |  |
|  |  |  |  |  |  |  |  |
|  |  |  |  |  |  |  |  |
|  |  |  |  |  |  |  |  |
|  |  |  |  |  |  |  |  |

## 18 EXERCISE

| DATE *(   ) | WEIGHT | REPS | WEIGHT | REPS | WEIGHT | REPS |
|---|---|---|---|---|---|---|
| / | | | | | | |
| / | | | | | | |
| / | | | | | | |
| / | | | | | | |
| / | | | | | | |
| / | | | | | | |
| / | | | | | | |
| / | | | | | | |
| / | | | | | | |
| / | | | | | | |
| / | | | | | | |
| / | | | | | | |
| / | | | | | | |
| / | | | | | | |
| / | | | | | | |
| / | | | | | | |
| / | | | | | | |
| / | | | | | | |
| / | | | | | | |

| WEIGHT | REPS | WEIGHT | REPS | WEIGHT | REPS | WEIGHT | REPS |
|--------|------|--------|------|--------|------|--------|------|
|  |  |  |  |  |  |  |  |
|  |  |  |  |  |  |  |  |
|  |  |  |  |  |  |  |  |
|  |  |  |  |  |  |  |  |
|  |  |  |  |  |  |  |  |
|  |  |  |  |  |  |  |  |
|  |  |  |  |  |  |  |  |
|  |  |  |  |  |  |  |  |
|  |  |  |  |  |  |  |  |
|  |  |  |  |  |  |  |  |
|  |  |  |  |  |  |  |  |
|  |  |  |  |  |  |  |  |
|  |  |  |  |  |  |  |  |
|  |  |  |  |  |  |  |  |
|  |  |  |  |  |  |  |  |
|  |  |  |  |  |  |  |  |
|  |  |  |  |  |  |  |  |
|  |  |  |  |  |  |  |  |
|  |  |  |  |  |  |  |  |

**19** EXERCISE

| DATE *( ) | WEIGHT | REPS | WEIGHT | REPS | WEIGHT | REPS |
|-----------|--------|------|--------|------|--------|------|
| / | | | | | | |
| / | | | | | | |
| / | | | | | | |
| / | | | | | | |
| / | | | | | | |
| / | | | | | | |
| / | | | | | | |
| / | | | | | | |
| / | | | | | | |
| / | | | | | | |
| / | | | | | | |
| / | | | | | | |
| / | | | | | | |
| / | | | | | | |
| / | | | | | | |
| / | | | | | | |
| / | | | | | | |
| / | | | | | | |
| / | | | | | | |

| WEIGHT | REPS | WEIGHT | REPS | WEIGHT | REPS | WEIGHT | REPS |
|---|---|---|---|---|---|---|---|
|  |  |  |  |  |  |  |  |
|  |  |  |  |  |  |  |  |
|  |  |  |  |  |  |  |  |
|  |  |  |  |  |  |  |  |
|  |  |  |  |  |  |  |  |
|  |  |  |  |  |  |  |  |
|  |  |  |  |  |  |  |  |
|  |  |  |  |  |  |  |  |
|  |  |  |  |  |  |  |  |
|  |  |  |  |  |  |  |  |
|  |  |  |  |  |  |  |  |
|  |  |  |  |  |  |  |  |
|  |  |  |  |  |  |  |  |
|  |  |  |  |  |  |  |  |
|  |  |  |  |  |  |  |  |
|  |  |  |  |  |  |  |  |
|  |  |  |  |  |  |  |  |
|  |  |  |  |  |  |  |  |
|  |  |  |  |  |  |  |  |

## 20 EXERCISE

| DATE *( ) | WEIGHT | REPS | WEIGHT | REPS | WEIGHT | REPS |
|---|---|---|---|---|---|---|
| / | | | | | | |
| / | | | | | | |
| / | | | | | | |
| / | | | | | | |
| / | | | | | | |
| / | | | | | | |
| / | | | | | | |
| / | | | | | | |
| / | | | | | | |
| / | | | | | | |
| / | | | | | | |
| / | | | | | | |
| / | | | | | | |
| / | | | | | | |
| / | | | | | | |
| / | | | | | | |
| / | | | | | | |
| / | | | | | | |
| / | | | | | | |

| WEIGHT | REPS | WEIGHT | REPS | WEIGHT | REPS | WEIGHT | REPS |
|---|---|---|---|---|---|---|---|
| | | | | | | | |
| | | | | | | | |
| | | | | | | | |
| | | | | | | | |
| | | | | | | | |
| | | | | | | | |
| | | | | | | | |
| | | | | | | | |
| | | | | | | | |
| | | | | | | | |
| | | | | | | | |
| | | | | | | | |
| | | | | | | | |
| | | | | | | | |
| | | | | | | | |
| | | | | | | | |
| | | | | | | | |
| | | | | | | | |
| | | | | | | | |
| | | | | | | | |

**21** EXERCISE

| DATE *(  ) | WEIGHT | REPS | WEIGHT | REPS | WEIGHT | REPS |
|---|---|---|---|---|---|---|
| / | | | | | | |
| / | | | | | | |
| / | | | | | | |
| / | | | | | | |
| / | | | | | | |
| / | | | | | | |
| / | | | | | | |
| / | | | | | | |
| / | | | | | | |
| / | | | | | | |
| / | | | | | | |
| / | | | | | | |
| / | | | | | | |
| / | | | | | | |
| / | | | | | | |
| / | | | | | | |
| / | | | | | | |
| / | | | | | | |
| / | | | | | | |

| WEIGHT | REPS | WEIGHT | REPS | WEIGHT | REPS | WEIGHT | REPS |
|--------|------|--------|------|--------|------|--------|------|
|        |      |        |      |        |      |        |      |
|        |      |        |      |        |      |        |      |
|        |      |        |      |        |      |        |      |
|        |      |        |      |        |      |        |      |
|        |      |        |      |        |      |        |      |
|        |      |        |      |        |      |        |      |
|        |      |        |      |        |      |        |      |
|        |      |        |      |        |      |        |      |
|        |      |        |      |        |      |        |      |
|        |      |        |      |        |      |        |      |
|        |      |        |      |        |      |        |      |
|        |      |        |      |        |      |        |      |
|        |      |        |      |        |      |        |      |
|        |      |        |      |        |      |        |      |
|        |      |        |      |        |      |        |      |
|        |      |        |      |        |      |        |      |
|        |      |        |      |        |      |        |      |
|        |      |        |      |        |      |        |      |
|        |      |        |      |        |      |        |      |

**EXERCISE**

| DATE *(  ) | WEIGHT | REPS | WEIGHT | REPS | WEIGHT | REPS |
|---|---|---|---|---|---|---|
| / | | | | | | |
| / | | | | | | |
| / | | | | | | |
| / | | | | | | |
| / | | | | | | |
| / | | | | | | |
| / | | | | | | |
| / | | | | | | |
| / | | | | | | |
| / | | | | | | |
| / | | | | | | |
| / | | | | | | |
| / | | | | | | |
| / | | | | | | |
| / | | | | | | |
| / | | | | | | |
| / | | | | | | |
| / | | | | | | |
| / | | | | | | |

| WEIGHT | REPS | WEIGHT | REPS | WEIGHT | REPS | WEIGHT | REPS |
|---|---|---|---|---|---|---|---|
|  |  |  |  |  |  |  |  |
|  |  |  |  |  |  |  |  |
|  |  |  |  |  |  |  |  |
|  |  |  |  |  |  |  |  |
|  |  |  |  |  |  |  |  |
|  |  |  |  |  |  |  |  |
|  |  |  |  |  |  |  |  |
|  |  |  |  |  |  |  |  |
|  |  |  |  |  |  |  |  |
|  |  |  |  |  |  |  |  |
|  |  |  |  |  |  |  |  |
|  |  |  |  |  |  |  |  |
|  |  |  |  |  |  |  |  |
|  |  |  |  |  |  |  |  |
|  |  |  |  |  |  |  |  |
|  |  |  |  |  |  |  |  |
|  |  |  |  |  |  |  |  |
|  |  |  |  |  |  |  |  |
|  |  |  |  |  |  |  |  |

## 23     EXERCISE

| DATE *(   ) | WEIGHT | REPS | WEIGHT | REPS | WEIGHT | REPS |
|---|---|---|---|---|---|---|
| / | | | | | | |
| / | | | | | | |
| / | | | | | | |
| / | | | | | | |
| / | | | | | | |
| / | | | | | | |
| / | | | | | | |
| / | | | | | | |
| / | | | | | | |
| / | | | | | | |
| / | | | | | | |
| / | | | | | | |
| / | | | | | | |
| / | | | | | | |
| / | | | | | | |
| / | | | | | | |
| / | | | | | | |
| / | | | | | | |
| / | | | | | | |

| WEIGHT | REPS | WEIGHT | REPS | WEIGHT | REPS | WEIGHT | REPS |
|--------|------|--------|------|--------|------|--------|------|
|        |      |        |      |        |      |        |      |
|        |      |        |      |        |      |        |      |
|        |      |        |      |        |      |        |      |
|        |      |        |      |        |      |        |      |
|        |      |        |      |        |      |        |      |
|        |      |        |      |        |      |        |      |
|        |      |        |      |        |      |        |      |
|        |      |        |      |        |      |        |      |
|        |      |        |      |        |      |        |      |
|        |      |        |      |        |      |        |      |
|        |      |        |      |        |      |        |      |
|        |      |        |      |        |      |        |      |
|        |      |        |      |        |      |        |      |
|        |      |        |      |        |      |        |      |
|        |      |        |      |        |      |        |      |
|        |      |        |      |        |      |        |      |
|        |      |        |      |        |      |        |      |
|        |      |        |      |        |      |        |      |
|        |      |        |      |        |      |        |      |

**EXERCISE**

| DATE *( ) | WEIGHT | REPS | WEIGHT | REPS | WEIGHT | REPS |
|-----------|--------|------|--------|------|--------|------|
| / | | | | | | |
| / | | | | | | |
| / | | | | | | |
| / | | | | | | |
| / | | | | | | |
| / | | | | | | |
| / | | | | | | |
| / | | | | | | |
| / | | | | | | |
| / | | | | | | |
| / | | | | | | |
| / | | | | | | |
| / | | | | | | |
| / | | | | | | |
| / | | | | | | |
| / | | | | | | |
| / | | | | | | |
| / | | | | | | |
| / | | | | | | |

| WEIGHT | REPS | WEIGHT | REPS | WEIGHT | REPS | WEIGHT | REPS |
|--------|------|--------|------|--------|------|--------|------|
|  |  |  |  |  |  |  |  |
|  |  |  |  |  |  |  |  |
|  |  |  |  |  |  |  |  |
|  |  |  |  |  |  |  |  |
|  |  |  |  |  |  |  |  |
|  |  |  |  |  |  |  |  |
|  |  |  |  |  |  |  |  |
|  |  |  |  |  |  |  |  |
|  |  |  |  |  |  |  |  |
|  |  |  |  |  |  |  |  |
|  |  |  |  |  |  |  |  |
|  |  |  |  |  |  |  |  |
|  |  |  |  |  |  |  |  |
|  |  |  |  |  |  |  |  |
|  |  |  |  |  |  |  |  |
|  |  |  |  |  |  |  |  |
|  |  |  |  |  |  |  |  |
|  |  |  |  |  |  |  |  |
|  |  |  |  |  |  |  |  |

## 25

**EXERCISE**

| DATE *( ) | WEIGHT | REPS | WEIGHT | REPS | WEIGHT | REPS |
|-----------|--------|------|--------|------|--------|------|
| / | | | | | | |
| / | | | | | | |
| / | | | | | | |
| / | | | | | | |
| / | | | | | | |
| / | | | | | | |
| / | | | | | | |
| / | | | | | | |
| / | | | | | | |
| / | | | | | | |
| / | | | | | | |
| / | | | | | | |
| / | | | | | | |
| / | | | | | | |
| / | | | | | | |
| / | | | | | | |
| / | | | | | | |
| / | | | | | | |
| / | | | | | | |

| WEIGHT | REPS | WEIGHT | REPS | WEIGHT | REPS | WEIGHT | REPS |
|---|---|---|---|---|---|---|---|
|  |  |  |  |  |  |  |  |
|  |  |  |  |  |  |  |  |
|  |  |  |  |  |  |  |  |
|  |  |  |  |  |  |  |  |
|  |  |  |  |  |  |  |  |
|  |  |  |  |  |  |  |  |
|  |  |  |  |  |  |  |  |
|  |  |  |  |  |  |  |  |
|  |  |  |  |  |  |  |  |
|  |  |  |  |  |  |  |  |
|  |  |  |  |  |  |  |  |
|  |  |  |  |  |  |  |  |
|  |  |  |  |  |  |  |  |
|  |  |  |  |  |  |  |  |
|  |  |  |  |  |  |  |  |
|  |  |  |  |  |  |  |  |
|  |  |  |  |  |  |  |  |
|  |  |  |  |  |  |  |  |
|  |  |  |  |  |  |  |  |

## 26 EXERCISE

| DATE *(    ) | WEIGHT | REPS | WEIGHT | REPS | WEIGHT | REPS |
|---|---|---|---|---|---|---|
| / | | | | | | |
| / | | | | | | |
| / | | | | | | |
| / | | | | | | |
| / | | | | | | |
| / | | | | | | |
| / | | | | | | |
| / | | | | | | |
| / | | | | | | |
| / | | | | | | |
| / | | | | | | |
| / | | | | | | |
| / | | | | | | |
| / | | | | | | |
| / | | | | | | |
| / | | | | | | |
| / | | | | | | |
| / | | | | | | |
| / | | | | | | |

| WEIGHT | REPS | WEIGHT | REPS | WEIGHT | REPS | WEIGHT | REPS |
|---|---|---|---|---|---|---|---|
|  |  |  |  |  |  |  |  |
|  |  |  |  |  |  |  |  |
|  |  |  |  |  |  |  |  |
|  |  |  |  |  |  |  |  |
|  |  |  |  |  |  |  |  |
|  |  |  |  |  |  |  |  |
|  |  |  |  |  |  |  |  |
|  |  |  |  |  |  |  |  |
|  |  |  |  |  |  |  |  |
|  |  |  |  |  |  |  |  |
|  |  |  |  |  |  |  |  |
|  |  |  |  |  |  |  |  |
|  |  |  |  |  |  |  |  |
|  |  |  |  |  |  |  |  |
|  |  |  |  |  |  |  |  |
|  |  |  |  |  |  |  |  |
|  |  |  |  |  |  |  |  |
|  |  |  |  |  |  |  |  |
|  |  |  |  |  |  |  |  |

## 27     EXERCISE

| DATE *(   ) | WEIGHT | REPS | WEIGHT | REPS | WEIGHT | REPS |
|---|---|---|---|---|---|---|
| / | | | | | | |
| / | | | | | | |
| / | | | | | | |
| / | | | | | | |
| / | | | | | | |
| / | | | | | | |
| / | | | | | | |
| / | | | | | | |
| / | | | | | | |
| / | | | | | | |
| / | | | | | | |
| / | | | | | | |
| / | | | | | | |
| / | | | | | | |
| / | | | | | | |
| / | | | | | | |
| / | | | | | | |
| / | | | | | | |
| / | | | | | | |

| WEIGHT | REPS | WEIGHT | REPS | WEIGHT | REPS | WEIGHT | REPS |
|--------|------|--------|------|--------|------|--------|------|
|  |  |  |  |  |  |  |  |
|  |  |  |  |  |  |  |  |
|  |  |  |  |  |  |  |  |
|  |  |  |  |  |  |  |  |
|  |  |  |  |  |  |  |  |
|  |  |  |  |  |  |  |  |
|  |  |  |  |  |  |  |  |
|  |  |  |  |  |  |  |  |
|  |  |  |  |  |  |  |  |
|  |  |  |  |  |  |  |  |
|  |  |  |  |  |  |  |  |
|  |  |  |  |  |  |  |  |
|  |  |  |  |  |  |  |  |
|  |  |  |  |  |  |  |  |
|  |  |  |  |  |  |  |  |
|  |  |  |  |  |  |  |  |
|  |  |  |  |  |  |  |  |
|  |  |  |  |  |  |  |  |
|  |  |  |  |  |  |  |  |

**28**    EXERCISE

| DATE *(    ) | WEIGHT | REPS | WEIGHT | REPS | WEIGHT | REPS |
|---|---|---|---|---|---|---|
| / | | | | | | |
| / | | | | | | |
| / | | | | | | |
| / | | | | | | |
| / | | | | | | |
| / | | | | | | |
| / | | | | | | |
| / | | | | | | |
| / | | | | | | |
| / | | | | | | |
| / | | | | | | |
| / | | | | | | |
| / | | | | | | |
| / | | | | | | |
| / | | | | | | |
| / | | | | | | |
| / | | | | | | |
| / | | | | | | |
| / | | | | | | |

| WEIGHT | REPS | WEIGHT | REPS | WEIGHT | REPS | WEIGHT | REPS |
|---|---|---|---|---|---|---|---|
|  |  |  |  |  |  |  |  |
|  |  |  |  |  |  |  |  |
|  |  |  |  |  |  |  |  |
|  |  |  |  |  |  |  |  |
|  |  |  |  |  |  |  |  |
|  |  |  |  |  |  |  |  |
|  |  |  |  |  |  |  |  |
|  |  |  |  |  |  |  |  |
|  |  |  |  |  |  |  |  |
|  |  |  |  |  |  |  |  |
|  |  |  |  |  |  |  |  |
|  |  |  |  |  |  |  |  |
|  |  |  |  |  |  |  |  |
|  |  |  |  |  |  |  |  |
|  |  |  |  |  |  |  |  |
|  |  |  |  |  |  |  |  |
|  |  |  |  |  |  |  |  |
|  |  |  |  |  |  |  |  |
|  |  |  |  |  |  |  |  |

## 29 EXERCISE

| DATE *(   ) | WEIGHT | REPS | WEIGHT | REPS | WEIGHT | REPS |
|---|---|---|---|---|---|---|
| / | | | | | | |
| / | | | | | | |
| / | | | | | | |
| / | | | | | | |
| / | | | | | | |
| / | | | | | | |
| / | | | | | | |
| / | | | | | | |
| / | | | | | | |
| / | | | | | | |
| / | | | | | | |
| / | | | | | | |
| / | | | | | | |
| / | | | | | | |
| / | | | | | | |
| / | | | | | | |
| / | | | | | | |
| / | | | | | | |
| / | | | | | | |

| WEIGHT | REPS | WEIGHT | REPS | WEIGHT | REPS | WEIGHT | REPS |
|--------|------|--------|------|--------|------|--------|------|
|        |      |        |      |        |      |        |      |
|        |      |        |      |        |      |        |      |
|        |      |        |      |        |      |        |      |
|        |      |        |      |        |      |        |      |
|        |      |        |      |        |      |        |      |
|        |      |        |      |        |      |        |      |
|        |      |        |      |        |      |        |      |
|        |      |        |      |        |      |        |      |
|        |      |        |      |        |      |        |      |
|        |      |        |      |        |      |        |      |
|        |      |        |      |        |      |        |      |
|        |      |        |      |        |      |        |      |
|        |      |        |      |        |      |        |      |
|        |      |        |      |        |      |        |      |
|        |      |        |      |        |      |        |      |
|        |      |        |      |        |      |        |      |
|        |      |        |      |        |      |        |      |
|        |      |        |      |        |      |        |      |
|        |      |        |      |        |      |        |      |

**EXERCISE**

| DATE *( ) | WEIGHT | REPS | WEIGHT | REPS | WEIGHT | REPS |
|---|---|---|---|---|---|---|
| / | | | | | | |
| / | | | | | | |
| / | | | | | | |
| / | | | | | | |
| / | | | | | | |
| / | | | | | | |
| / | | | | | | |
| / | | | | | | |
| / | | | | | | |
| / | | | | | | |
| / | | | | | | |
| / | | | | | | |
| / | | | | | | |
| / | | | | | | |
| / | | | | | | |
| / | | | | | | |
| / | | | | | | |
| / | | | | | | |
| / | | | | | | |

| WEIGHT | REPS | WEIGHT | REPS | WEIGHT | REPS | WEIGHT | REPS |
|---|---|---|---|---|---|---|---|
|  |  |  |  |  |  |  |  |
|  |  |  |  |  |  |  |  |
|  |  |  |  |  |  |  |  |
|  |  |  |  |  |  |  |  |
|  |  |  |  |  |  |  |  |
|  |  |  |  |  |  |  |  |
|  |  |  |  |  |  |  |  |
|  |  |  |  |  |  |  |  |
|  |  |  |  |  |  |  |  |
|  |  |  |  |  |  |  |  |
|  |  |  |  |  |  |  |  |
|  |  |  |  |  |  |  |  |
|  |  |  |  |  |  |  |  |
|  |  |  |  |  |  |  |  |
|  |  |  |  |  |  |  |  |
|  |  |  |  |  |  |  |  |
|  |  |  |  |  |  |  |  |
|  |  |  |  |  |  |  |  |
|  |  |  |  |  |  |  |  |

**31**  EXERCISE

| DATE *( ) | WEIGHT | REPS | WEIGHT | REPS | WEIGHT | REPS |
|-----------|--------|------|--------|------|--------|------|
| / | | | | | | |
| / | | | | | | |
| / | | | | | | |
| / | | | | | | |
| / | | | | | | |
| / | | | | | | |
| / | | | | | | |
| / | | | | | | |
| / | | | | | | |
| / | | | | | | |
| / | | | | | | |
| / | | | | | | |
| / | | | | | | |
| / | | | | | | |
| / | | | | | | |
| / | | | | | | |
| / | | | | | | |
| / | | | | | | |
| / | | | | | | |

| WEIGHT | REPS | WEIGHT | REPS | WEIGHT | REPS | WEIGHT | REPS |
|--------|------|--------|------|--------|------|--------|------|
|  |  |  |  |  |  |  |  |
|  |  |  |  |  |  |  |  |
|  |  |  |  |  |  |  |  |
|  |  |  |  |  |  |  |  |
|  |  |  |  |  |  |  |  |
|  |  |  |  |  |  |  |  |
|  |  |  |  |  |  |  |  |
|  |  |  |  |  |  |  |  |
|  |  |  |  |  |  |  |  |
|  |  |  |  |  |  |  |  |
|  |  |  |  |  |  |  |  |
|  |  |  |  |  |  |  |  |
|  |  |  |  |  |  |  |  |
|  |  |  |  |  |  |  |  |
|  |  |  |  |  |  |  |  |
|  |  |  |  |  |  |  |  |
|  |  |  |  |  |  |  |  |
|  |  |  |  |  |  |  |  |
|  |  |  |  |  |  |  |  |

**32**  EXERCISE

| DATE *( ) | WEIGHT | REPS | WEIGHT | REPS | WEIGHT | REPS |
|---|---|---|---|---|---|---|
| / | | | | | | |
| / | | | | | | |
| / | | | | | | |
| / | | | | | | |
| / | | | | | | |
| / | | | | | | |
| / | | | | | | |
| / | | | | | | |
| / | | | | | | |
| / | | | | | | |
| / | | | | | | |
| / | | | | | | |
| / | | | | | | |
| / | | | | | | |
| / | | | | | | |
| / | | | | | | |
| / | | | | | | |
| / | | | | | | |
| / | | | | | | |

| WEIGHT | REPS | WEIGHT | REPS | WEIGHT | REPS | WEIGHT | REPS |
|---|---|---|---|---|---|---|---|
| | | | | | | | |
| | | | | | | | |
| | | | | | | | |
| | | | | | | | |
| | | | | | | | |
| | | | | | | | |
| | | | | | | | |
| | | | | | | | |
| | | | | | | | |
| | | | | | | | |
| | | | | | | | |
| | | | | | | | |
| | | | | | | | |
| | | | | | | | |
| | | | | | | | |
| | | | | | | | |
| | | | | | | | |
| | | | | | | | |
| | | | | | | | |

## 33

EXERCISE

| DATE *(   ) | WEIGHT | REPS | WEIGHT | REPS | WEIGHT | REPS |
|---|---|---|---|---|---|---|
| / | | | | | | |
| / | | | | | | |
| / | | | | | | |
| / | | | | | | |
| / | | | | | | |
| / | | | | | | |
| / | | | | | | |
| / | | | | | | |
| / | | | | | | |
| / | | | | | | |
| / | | | | | | |
| / | | | | | | |
| / | | | | | | |
| / | | | | | | |
| / | | | | | | |
| / | | | | | | |
| / | | | | | | |
| / | | | | | | |
| / | | | | | | |

| WEIGHT | REPS | WEIGHT | REPS | WEIGHT | REPS | WEIGHT | REPS |
|--------|------|--------|------|--------|------|--------|------|
|  |  |  |  |  |  |  |  |
|  |  |  |  |  |  |  |  |
|  |  |  |  |  |  |  |  |
|  |  |  |  |  |  |  |  |
|  |  |  |  |  |  |  |  |
|  |  |  |  |  |  |  |  |
|  |  |  |  |  |  |  |  |
|  |  |  |  |  |  |  |  |
|  |  |  |  |  |  |  |  |
|  |  |  |  |  |  |  |  |
|  |  |  |  |  |  |  |  |
|  |  |  |  |  |  |  |  |
|  |  |  |  |  |  |  |  |
|  |  |  |  |  |  |  |  |
|  |  |  |  |  |  |  |  |
|  |  |  |  |  |  |  |  |
|  |  |  |  |  |  |  |  |
|  |  |  |  |  |  |  |  |
|  |  |  |  |  |  |  |  |

**EXERCISE**

| DATE *( ) | WEIGHT | REPS | WEIGHT | REPS | WEIGHT | REPS |
|---|---|---|---|---|---|---|
| / | | | | | | |
| / | | | | | | |
| / | | | | | | |
| / | | | | | | |
| / | | | | | | |
| / | | | | | | |
| / | | | | | | |
| / | | | | | | |
| / | | | | | | |
| / | | | | | | |
| / | | | | | | |
| / | | | | | | |
| / | | | | | | |
| / | | | | | | |
| / | | | | | | |
| / | | | | | | |
| / | | | | | | |
| / | | | | | | |
| / | | | | | | |

| WEIGHT | REPS | WEIGHT | REPS | WEIGHT | REPS | WEIGHT | REPS |
|--------|------|--------|------|--------|------|--------|------|
|        |      |        |      |        |      |        |      |
|        |      |        |      |        |      |        |      |
|        |      |        |      |        |      |        |      |
|        |      |        |      |        |      |        |      |
|        |      |        |      |        |      |        |      |
|        |      |        |      |        |      |        |      |
|        |      |        |      |        |      |        |      |
|        |      |        |      |        |      |        |      |
|        |      |        |      |        |      |        |      |
|        |      |        |      |        |      |        |      |
|        |      |        |      |        |      |        |      |
|        |      |        |      |        |      |        |      |
|        |      |        |      |        |      |        |      |
|        |      |        |      |        |      |        |      |
|        |      |        |      |        |      |        |      |
|        |      |        |      |        |      |        |      |
|        |      |        |      |        |      |        |      |
|        |      |        |      |        |      |        |      |
|        |      |        |      |        |      |        |      |

## 35 EXERCISE

| DATE *( ) | WEIGHT | REPS | WEIGHT | REPS | WEIGHT | REPS |
|-----------|--------|------|--------|------|--------|------|
| / | | | | | | |
| / | | | | | | |
| / | | | | | | |
| / | | | | | | |
| / | | | | | | |
| / | | | | | | |
| / | | | | | | |
| / | | | | | | |
| / | | | | | | |
| / | | | | | | |
| / | | | | | | |
| / | | | | | | |
| / | | | | | | |
| / | | | | | | |
| / | | | | | | |
| / | | | | | | |
| / | | | | | | |
| / | | | | | | |
| / | | | | | | |

| WEIGHT | REPS | WEIGHT | REPS | WEIGHT | REPS | WEIGHT | REPS |
|--------|------|--------|------|--------|------|--------|------|
|        |      |        |      |        |      |        |      |
|        |      |        |      |        |      |        |      |
|        |      |        |      |        |      |        |      |
|        |      |        |      |        |      |        |      |
|        |      |        |      |        |      |        |      |
|        |      |        |      |        |      |        |      |
|        |      |        |      |        |      |        |      |
|        |      |        |      |        |      |        |      |
|        |      |        |      |        |      |        |      |
|        |      |        |      |        |      |        |      |
|        |      |        |      |        |      |        |      |
|        |      |        |      |        |      |        |      |
|        |      |        |      |        |      |        |      |
|        |      |        |      |        |      |        |      |
|        |      |        |      |        |      |        |      |
|        |      |        |      |        |      |        |      |
|        |      |        |      |        |      |        |      |
|        |      |        |      |        |      |        |      |
|        |      |        |      |        |      |        |      |

## 36     EXERCISE

| DATE *( ) | WEIGHT | REPS | WEIGHT | REPS | WEIGHT | REPS |
|---|---|---|---|---|---|---|
| / | | | | | | |
| / | | | | | | |
| / | | | | | | |
| / | | | | | | |
| / | | | | | | |
| / | | | | | | |
| / | | | | | | |
| / | | | | | | |
| / | | | | | | |
| / | | | | | | |
| / | | | | | | |
| / | | | | | | |
| / | | | | | | |
| / | | | | | | |
| / | | | | | | |
| / | | | | | | |
| / | | | | | | |
| / | | | | | | |
| / | | | | | | |

| WEIGHT | REPS | WEIGHT | REPS | WEIGHT | REPS | WEIGHT | REPS |
|---|---|---|---|---|---|---|---|
|  |  |  |  |  |  |  |  |
|  |  |  |  |  |  |  |  |
|  |  |  |  |  |  |  |  |
|  |  |  |  |  |  |  |  |
|  |  |  |  |  |  |  |  |
|  |  |  |  |  |  |  |  |
|  |  |  |  |  |  |  |  |
|  |  |  |  |  |  |  |  |
|  |  |  |  |  |  |  |  |
|  |  |  |  |  |  |  |  |
|  |  |  |  |  |  |  |  |
|  |  |  |  |  |  |  |  |
|  |  |  |  |  |  |  |  |
|  |  |  |  |  |  |  |  |
|  |  |  |  |  |  |  |  |
|  |  |  |  |  |  |  |  |
|  |  |  |  |  |  |  |  |
|  |  |  |  |  |  |  |  |
|  |  |  |  |  |  |  |  |

**37** EXERCISE

| DATE *(   ) | WEIGHT | REPS | WEIGHT | REPS | WEIGHT | REPS |
|---|---|---|---|---|---|---|
| / | | | | | | |
| / | | | | | | |
| / | | | | | | |
| / | | | | | | |
| / | | | | | | |
| / | | | | | | |
| / | | | | | | |
| / | | | | | | |
| / | | | | | | |
| / | | | | | | |
| / | | | | | | |
| / | | | | | | |
| / | | | | | | |
| / | | | | | | |
| / | | | | | | |
| / | | | | | | |
| / | | | | | | |
| / | | | | | | |
| / | | | | | | |

| WEIGHT | REPS | WEIGHT | REPS | WEIGHT | REPS | WEIGHT | REPS |
|--------|------|--------|------|--------|------|--------|------|
|  |  |  |  |  |  |  |  |
|  |  |  |  |  |  |  |  |
|  |  |  |  |  |  |  |  |
|  |  |  |  |  |  |  |  |
|  |  |  |  |  |  |  |  |
|  |  |  |  |  |  |  |  |
|  |  |  |  |  |  |  |  |
|  |  |  |  |  |  |  |  |
|  |  |  |  |  |  |  |  |
|  |  |  |  |  |  |  |  |
|  |  |  |  |  |  |  |  |
|  |  |  |  |  |  |  |  |
|  |  |  |  |  |  |  |  |
|  |  |  |  |  |  |  |  |
|  |  |  |  |  |  |  |  |
|  |  |  |  |  |  |  |  |
|  |  |  |  |  |  |  |  |
|  |  |  |  |  |  |  |  |
|  |  |  |  |  |  |  |  |

**38**     **EXERCISE**

| DATE *(  ) | WEIGHT | REPS | WEIGHT | REPS | WEIGHT | REPS |
|---|---|---|---|---|---|---|
| / | | | | | | |
| / | | | | | | |
| / | | | | | | |
| / | | | | | | |
| / | | | | | | |
| / | | | | | | |
| / | | | | | | |
| / | | | | | | |
| / | | | | | | |
| / | | | | | | |
| / | | | | | | |
| / | | | | | | |
| / | | | | | | |
| / | | | | | | |
| / | | | | | | |
| / | | | | | | |
| / | | | | | | |
| / | | | | | | |

| WEIGHT | REPS | WEIGHT | REPS | WEIGHT | REPS | WEIGHT | REPS |
|--------|------|--------|------|--------|------|--------|------|
|        |      |        |      |        |      |        |      |
|        |      |        |      |        |      |        |      |
|        |      |        |      |        |      |        |      |
|        |      |        |      |        |      |        |      |
|        |      |        |      |        |      |        |      |
|        |      |        |      |        |      |        |      |
|        |      |        |      |        |      |        |      |
|        |      |        |      |        |      |        |      |
|        |      |        |      |        |      |        |      |
|        |      |        |      |        |      |        |      |
|        |      |        |      |        |      |        |      |
|        |      |        |      |        |      |        |      |
|        |      |        |      |        |      |        |      |
|        |      |        |      |        |      |        |      |
|        |      |        |      |        |      |        |      |
|        |      |        |      |        |      |        |      |
|        |      |        |      |        |      |        |      |
|        |      |        |      |        |      |        |      |
|        |      |        |      |        |      |        |      |

**EXERCISE**

| DATE *( ) | WEIGHT | REPS | WEIGHT | REPS | WEIGHT | REPS |
|---|---|---|---|---|---|---|
| / | | | | | | |
| / | | | | | | |
| / | | | | | | |
| / | | | | | | |
| / | | | | | | |
| / | | | | | | |
| / | | | | | | |
| / | | | | | | |
| / | | | | | | |
| / | | | | | | |
| / | | | | | | |
| / | | | | | | |
| / | | | | | | |
| / | | | | | | |
| / | | | | | | |
| / | | | | | | |
| / | | | | | | |
| / | | | | | | |
| / | | | | | | |

| WEIGHT | REPS | WEIGHT | REPS | WEIGHT | REPS | WEIGHT | REPS |
|--------|------|--------|------|--------|------|--------|------|
|        |      |        |      |        |      |        |      |
|        |      |        |      |        |      |        |      |
|        |      |        |      |        |      |        |      |
|        |      |        |      |        |      |        |      |
|        |      |        |      |        |      |        |      |
|        |      |        |      |        |      |        |      |
|        |      |        |      |        |      |        |      |
|        |      |        |      |        |      |        |      |
|        |      |        |      |        |      |        |      |
|        |      |        |      |        |      |        |      |
|        |      |        |      |        |      |        |      |
|        |      |        |      |        |      |        |      |
|        |      |        |      |        |      |        |      |
|        |      |        |      |        |      |        |      |
|        |      |        |      |        |      |        |      |
|        |      |        |      |        |      |        |      |
|        |      |        |      |        |      |        |      |
|        |      |        |      |        |      |        |      |
|        |      |        |      |        |      |        |      |

## 40 EXERCISE

| DATE *( ) | WEIGHT | REPS | WEIGHT | REPS | WEIGHT | REPS |
|-----------|--------|------|--------|------|--------|------|
| / | | | | | | |
| / | | | | | | |
| / | | | | | | |
| / | | | | | | |
| / | | | | | | |
| / | | | | | | |
| / | | | | | | |
| / | | | | | | |
| / | | | | | | |
| / | | | | | | |
| / | | | | | | |
| / | | | | | | |
| / | | | | | | |
| / | | | | | | |
| / | | | | | | |
| / | | | | | | |
| / | | | | | | |
| / | | | | | | |
| / | | | | | | |

| WEIGHT | REPS | WEIGHT | REPS | WEIGHT | REPS | WEIGHT | REPS |
|---|---|---|---|---|---|---|---|
| | | | | | | | |
| | | | | | | | |
| | | | | | | | |
| | | | | | | | |
| | | | | | | | |
| | | | | | | | |
| | | | | | | | |
| | | | | | | | |
| | | | | | | | |
| | | | | | | | |
| | | | | | | | |
| | | | | | | | |
| | | | | | | | |
| | | | | | | | |
| | | | | | | | |
| | | | | | | | |
| | | | | | | | |
| | | | | | | | |
| | | | | | | | |

# ROUTINES

| PAGE | EXERCISE | SETS | PAGE | EXERCISE | SETS |
|------|----------|------|------|----------|------|
|      |          |      |      |          |      |
|      |          |      |      |          |      |
|      |          |      |      |          |      |
|      |          |      |      |          |      |
|      |          |      |      |          |      |
|      |          |      |      |          |      |
|      |          |      |      |          |      |

| PAGE | EXERCISE | SETS | PAGE | EXERCISE | SETS |
|------|----------|------|------|----------|------|
|      |          |      |      |          |      |
|      |          |      |      |          |      |
|      |          |      |      |          |      |
|      |          |      |      |          |      |
|      |          |      |      |          |      |
|      |          |      |      |          |      |
|      |          |      |      |          |      |

| PAGE | EXERCISE | SETS | PAGE | EXERCISE | SETS |
|------|----------|------|------|----------|------|
|      |          |      |      |          |      |
|      |          |      |      |          |      |
|      |          |      |      |          |      |
|      |          |      |      |          |      |
|      |          |      |      |          |      |
|      |          |      |      |          |      |
|      |          |      |      |          |      |

| PAGE | EXERCISE | SETS | PAGE | EXERCISE | SETS |
|------|----------|------|------|----------|------|
|      |          |      |      |          |      |
|      |          |      |      |          |      |
|      |          |      |      |          |      |
|      |          |      |      |          |      |
|      |          |      |      |          |      |
|      |          |      |      |          |      |
|      |          |      |      |          |      |

# ROUTINES

| PAGE | EXERCISE | SETS | | PAGE | EXERCISE | SETS |
|------|----------|------|---|------|----------|------|
| | | | | | | |
| | | | | | | |
| | | | | | | |
| | | | | | | |
| | | | | | | |
| | | | | | | |
| | | | | | | |

| PAGE | EXERCISE | SETS | | PAGE | EXERCISE | SETS |
|------|----------|------|---|------|----------|------|
| | | | | | | |
| | | | | | | |
| | | | | | | |
| | | | | | | |
| | | | | | | |
| | | | | | | |
| | | | | | | |

|  | PAGE | EXERCISE | SETS |  | PAGE | EXERCISE | SETS |
|---|---|---|---|---|---|---|---|
| ◯ |  |  | ☐ | ◯ |  |  | ☐ |
| ◯ |  |  | ☐ | ◯ |  |  | ☐ |
| ◯ |  |  | ☐ | ◯ |  |  | ☐ |
| ◯ |  |  | ☐ | ◯ |  |  | ☐ |
| ◯ |  |  | ☐ | ◯ |  |  | ☐ |
| ◯ |  |  | ☐ | ◯ |  |  | ☐ |
| ◯ |  |  | ☐ | ◯ |  |  | ☐ |

|  | PAGE | EXERCISE | SETS |  | PAGE | EXERCISE | SETS |
|---|---|---|---|---|---|---|---|
| ◯ |  |  | ☐ | ◯ |  |  | ☐ |
| ◯ |  |  | ☐ | ◯ |  |  | ☐ |
| ◯ |  |  | ☐ | ◯ |  |  | ☐ |
| ◯ |  |  | ☐ | ◯ |  |  | ☐ |
| ◯ |  |  | ☐ | ◯ |  |  | ☐ |
| ◯ |  |  | ☐ | ◯ |  |  | ☐ |
| ◯ |  |  | ☐ | ◯ |  |  | ☐ |

# ROUTINES

| PAGE | EXERCISE | SETS | | PAGE | EXERCISE | SETS |
|------|----------|------|---|------|----------|------|
| | | | | | | |
| | | | | | | |
| | | | | | | |
| | | | | | | |
| | | | | | | |
| | | | | | | |
| | | | | | | |

| PAGE | EXERCISE | SETS | | PAGE | EXERCISE | SETS |
|------|----------|------|---|------|----------|------|
| | | | | | | |
| | | | | | | |
| | | | | | | |
| | | | | | | |
| | | | | | | |
| | | | | | | |
| | | | | | | |

| PAGE | EXERCISE | SETS | PAGE | EXERCISE | SETS |
|------|----------|------|------|----------|------|
|      |          |      |      |          |      |
|      |          |      |      |          |      |
|      |          |      |      |          |      |
|      |          |      |      |          |      |
|      |          |      |      |          |      |
|      |          |      |      |          |      |
|      |          |      |      |          |      |

| PAGE | EXERCISE | SETS | PAGE | EXERCISE | SETS |
|------|----------|------|------|----------|------|
|      |          |      |      |          |      |
|      |          |      |      |          |      |
|      |          |      |      |          |      |
|      |          |      |      |          |      |
|      |          |      |      |          |      |
|      |          |      |      |          |      |
|      |          |      |      |          |      |

Made in the USA
San Bernardino, CA
21 December 2019

62168228R00053